Caught in the Light

poems by

Erika D. Walker

Finishing Line Press
Georgetown, Kentucky

Caught in the Light

Copyright © 2020 by Erika D. Walker
ISBN 978-1-64662-354-9 First Edition
All rights reserved under International and Pan-American Copyright Conventions. No part of this book may be reproduced in any manner whatsoever without written permission from the publisher, except in the case of brief quotations embodied in critical articles and reviews.

ACKNOWLEDGMENTS

I am grateful to the editors of the following publications for first publishing these poems:

Bird's Thumb: "To the Foxes"
Pulse: Voices from the Heart of Medicine: "Top of the Hill" and "First Saturday Night at the Nursing Home"
The Human Touch: Journal of Poetry, Prose, and Visual Art: "Father, How Will You Leave This World," "I ran away," "The Test"

Publisher: Leah Huete de Maines

Editor: Christen Kincaid

Cover Art: wingmar iStock ID 157195387

Author Photo: Vicki Kerr, Kerr Photography

Cover Design: Nancy Rice, tiny studio llc

Order online: www.finishinglinepress.com
also available on amazon.com

Author inquiries and mail orders:
Finishing Line Press
P. O. Box 1626
Georgetown, Kentucky 40324
U. S. A.

Table of Contents

I Wish I'd Asked Her More 1

Worse Things 2

I ran away 3

To the Bull Elk at the WMCA 4

Walk at Sunrise Ranch 5

Father, How Will You Leave This World? 6

Biography, Colorado 7

The Largest Hot Springs in the World 8

First Saturday Night at the Nursing Home 9

The Swallow 11

Pelican, Anna Maria Island 12

Top of the Hill 13

Winter Vigil 14

To the Foxes 15

Afterwards 16

My Secret 17

How Many Fields Have I Passed? 18

I See His Closet Still 19

The Test 20

Caught in the Light 21

Just for the Taking 22

My Best Kite Ever 23

Not Gone 24

As If 26

In loving memory of my father,
Gerald Steven Walker
1924 – 2006

Love is not consolation. It is light.
Simone Weil

I Wish I'd Asked Her More

Professor Marion wafts down the cool corridors
of her island home, jungle print caftan billows behind.
Two white Pekinese, like worried courtiers anxious
to please, puff and scuttle in her wake. Once
her student, now her friend, I swim in her pool,
read from her library, walk the beach at Lido Key.

Every day at 6 p.m., she presides over Happy Hour,
serves peanuts in small white bowls on a
red lacquered tray. *You spend the first half
of your life acquiring things*, she said, sipping
her drink, sea breeze warm on her patio.
A spouse, children, your profession, friends.

Then you spend the second half losing them. I wish
I'd asked her more, how you lose them, and especially—
how you survive. But like coquinas on the beach,
the conversation opened and closed before I realized it.
Loss seemed unimaginable that day, gin and tonic in hand,
the perfume of hibiscus over everything.

Worse Things

In winter, just after Christmas,
Father's cough did not stop. His cough
kept coming, a cough like drowning,

like boulders breaking, crashing
at the edge of the sea. He stayed
in bed for days, refused to eat.

Doctor said he wasn't too bad, sent him
home again. At night, Father rode
the cough and we both tried to sleep.

I told myself it was an ordinary day,
planned my sister's birthday party,
drove to the grocery store.

Alone in the kitchen, I sucked
long breaths, as if to breathe
for him. I told myself

the medicines were working,
that Father would be okay.
I started the soup, skinned

the chicken, plunged pink flesh
into boiling water. Down the hall,
he foamed and sputtered.

Dad. I shook his arm. *Dad.*
I raised my voice. *You are sleeping
too much. We're going back to the ER.*

He did not open his eyes, did not move.
There are worse things, he said,
than sleeping too much.

I ran away

from Father's strangled cough,
the crumpled bed, his dark room,

away from the gray face I wanted
to forget. I ran to the prairie,

where distant mountains do not end,
forever and ever, amen. A bitter winter

wind laid down the brown
grasses. Old snow settled

in shadows beside the empty lake,
a fractured map I could not read.

Feet pounded my prayer on frozen
ground: *don't let him die, don't let him die.*

From the top of the cottonwood
a blue heron rose on the wild wind,

great wings sliced the sky, lifted
past the tangled branch.

To the Bull Elk at the YMCA

In the last light of a late summer day
you came to the place you thought was home.

Down from high mountains, you followed
ancient trails, sought open meadow, but found

cabins and cars and clipped green lawn,
couples wandering with ice cream cones.

Wapiti, I say, *Wapiti. Raise
your great hoof, split this velvet fiction.*

You stand still as twilight—
and the sky turns to ash.

**

Did you see the elk?

Eyes wide in the night
faces wet with sweat

boys push past
pound up the stairs.

*It's wrong to throw a rock
at a wild animal,* said one

who trailed the rest, as if
to himself, as if—someone cared.

Walk at Sunrise Ranch

Rimrock valley slices wide
the October sky, yellow leaves,
like tattered prayer flags, brood
over grass bent low.

Wild turkeys bolt from deep
in the pines. Shadows come
to life, they flash across the field
intent on some secret urgency.

No big-breasted gobblers, these
foothill ruffians run like sun
on water. Their wild current
surprises my meditations.

I follow, but they vanish,
lost in the garden's cool
sanctuary. I hear them pass,
a small wind in dry leaves.

Father, How Will You Leave This World?

Will you lose your breath
forever, in this cough
that will not stop?

Will your heart give up, erupt
into a fury that launches you
into heaven?

At night, alone
in your house,
I wait.

Across town, wires
clipped to your chest,
you wait.

Machines measure
your oxygen, the nurse listens
for your beating heart.

I listen for the mountain's
breath, the song of the trout
we brought back for breakfast.

I remember cold mornings, how
you taught me to study the water,
feel for the faint tug on my line.

Biography, Colorado

I walk great-grandfather's land, the claim
he staked on the mountainside, home place

of elk, grizzly bear, mountain lion. Who was this man
who brought his bride west, raised six children

among columbine and ponderosa, his axe marks still
on the cabin's logs? My hand maps the tall grass

where their garden grew. I study the sky
from the hollow where the root cellar caved in.

Here is a place where wind begins a long way away,
like something you can't quite remember.

Here is a place where aspen trace deep water
and the scree scree of the hawk stops your blood.

Here is a place where dark means dark—
and the Milky Way still broods over the land.

The Largest Hot Springs Pool in the World

I glide in the night, in warm river
water cut from the Colorado, poured
into the pool. I fly and float, bird
and fish. My hands pull me past
divers and belly whoppers, laughing

Japanese tourists, past old men
walrusing on their backs, arms open
to the sky. In the deep end, light reflects
on dark water like melted music,
lovers entwine in shadows.

Before highways, this valley belonged
to rivers and mountains, to blue gill and bass,
to mule deer, bob cat, big horn sheep. Utes too
knew this healing place, rested in sweet scent
of willow and red mud, sky alive with stars.

Next morning, in the cool, twenty eagles
wheel across flat gray sky, as if nothing
had ever changed. Mist moves
over the water, like smoke
from an ancient fire.

First Saturday Night at the Nursing Home

I stare at my chicken patty,
the limp lettuce, pale tomato
sliver, open the small

mayonnaise packet, even though
I don't eat mayonnaise.
I pour my milk, set the carton

on the table, slide aside
the red Jell-O. If I don't look
up, I won't be where I am.

Father wears a blue dress shirt,
not his own, stares,
not speaking, not noticing

the shirt is buttoned wrong,
brown stain on the front.
His hair stands straight up

and wild, blown by some private
windstorm. A woman alone
at the next table, tied

to a wheelchair, howls
each breath, in and out,
low and loud, over and over.

I try to breathe outside of her breathing—
but I cannot. Not even the watery
Christmas carols pouring through

the dining room can drown
her out. I want to scream,
to shut this woman up. I want

to grab my father, spin
his wheelchair around,
take him back home, back

to last week, back to twenty years ago,
away from the chicken patty
that resists my knife.

The Swallow

A fierce wind scrapes
the prairie, a scrap

of a bird fights
to fly, struggles

up then down, tries to find
a door in the wall of wind

but she cannot advance.
Her wings beat and beat

their frantic pulse.
She hangs there,

a dark speck against
the steel November sky.

Pelican, Anna Maria Island

Summoned by the setting sun,
low and red above the sea,
I walk past the last house,

the tall pines, past
the sea oats, push into the wild
wind, my bare feet fighting

the wave's ragged edge. Sheltered
in the twilight, you stand
steadfast, unexpected as a stump.

Startled, I nearly fall. You do not
raise your great wings, do not break
your gaze, fixed on the far horizon.

What's wrong, why doesn't he fly?
He's dying, says an old man. *Can't we call*
someone? Take him to a doctor?

No. Nothing can be done.
In the morning he'll be gone.

I kneel in the cold sand, my mouth full of salt.
Keening gulls stitch the darkening sky,
rough water breaks over your solid feet.

Top of the Hill

It's as if you're at the top of a hill,
the doctor says. My father listens
from his hospital bed, a plastic tube

feeds him breath he can no longer take
for himself. *Each time you get sick,*
the doctor says, *you roll a little farther*

down the hill. His young face shines
above his white coat. I remember rolling
down green hills when I was young,

playing in the park where my father
played as a child. I laughed, loved
the bump and thrill, the smell

of summer grass. I raced my brother
to the top so we could fall again.
We can catch you, the doctor says

and looks away. *But we can never
get you back to the top of the hill.*
I see my father roll now, gather speed,

the ties of his hospital gown flailing
like small hands. The doctor and I
reach to catch him, grass stains

the doctor's coat, my fingernails fill
with mud. My father closes his eyes.
If he remembers hills, he does not say.

Winter Vigil

I finger the days, like small beads,
walk beside the frozen river. Crows

flare over blue ice. In silent cold,
I hear Father's walker, how it

lisps along gray carpet
as he pushes down the hall.

I shop for dinner, feel each onion,
choose this one over that. Find

six fine potatoes for soup.
I drive home from work, chop

carrots, call out my son's
spelling words, boil water.

I listen for the phone, afraid.
Has Father fallen? Or worse?

When I cannot sleep, I hear
his breath—wind trapped in a canyon.

To the Foxes

I just came to warn you,
the neighbor said, *foxes have moved in
since your father's been gone. We've seen*

*two prancing down the street. Kittens
and small dogs have disappeared. At night
they return to your father's back yard. Look,*

look, there in that hole. She spins
me around, points to the bushes. *I'm afraid,*
she says, her voice low. *My poodle*

*is afraid. He doesn't want to go outside.
Make sure you leave no windows open. Foxes
will invade your home.* I check

the cedar hedge, search the vinca, part
the tangled Virginia creeper curtain. Nothing
moves. No glittering eyes, no sharp teeth.

Fifty years ago the prairie was my back yard.
Lured by the meadow lark and the wild blue sky,
I played pioneer, safe in the smell of sage.

Cottonwoods long gone, strip
malls and suburbia silenced
the prairie. I too am afraid.

To the foxes, I say, *Go ahead,
eat a few poodles. That's the
least we can offer you.*

Afterwards

I walk through the door,
set my suitcase down
in the quiet house,
mail piled and sliding
off the kitchen table.

I start to call you,
Father, to tell you
we'd made it home.
Our flight was fine,
smooth sailing all the way.

I was going to tell you
that the pilot, somewhere over Iowa,
announced a boy's turtle was missing,
and how we laughed in the back
with the flight attendant.

And then
I remember.

My Secret

Where's my gray sweater?
Father would ask. He was hot,
then cold. *I don't know,* I'd reply,

it's here somewhere. We'd find it
buried in his recliner,
heaped on the floor, flung

over his walker where he'd put it
for safe keeping. I'd hold his sweater,
pretend not to notice the slow wander

of his hands as they tunneled
down the sleeves. When we left
his apartment, he'd ask,

Will I need my sweater?
I don't know, I'd reply,
why not bring it along?

Walking down the hall, he'd stop,
search for breath. I'd stroke his back,
smooth his sweater and wait.

After he died, I sat in his recliner,
leaned into his sweater's empty arms
and cried, tried to find his smell again.

I took it home, hid it in the bottom
of my drawer, hoping what was left
of him would not go away.

How Many Fields Have I Passed?

Snowy owl, blown off course,
is reported at the intersection
of Highways 1 and 9.

We drive south for an hour, seeking
this wayward migrant, late afternoon
sun in the belly of a gray sky, filled

with snow not yet fallen. We stand
in a farmer's field, backs to the wind,
scan brown stubble. *See the white spot?*

On the fifth telephone pole? The owl
swoops down, soars across the field,
wide white wings skim black earth.

Where is she now? See the church?
Look left. See what looks like a small
mound of snow? Through the scope,

I finally find her. Yellow eyes unblinking,
she grips frozen earth, as if this place
had always been home.

How many fields have I passed,
too fast, seeing only
plowed ground, scuffs of snow?

I See His Closet, Still

Father's snow boots
his golf shoes
Kenmore vacuum cleaner

black over coat
blue dress suit
brown bomber jacket

card table
poker chips
Maggie's Scrabble game

Air Force uniform
in a plastic bag

soft red plaid scarf
folded as he left it

yellow leather driving gloves
curled in the shape of his hands

The Test

First thing this morning,
I test myself again.
I hear my father
say my name
and, for a moment,
the world feels right.

But then, I'm not sure.
Did he say *Riki*,
a quick two beats
same tone or was it *Riki*,
a high pitch,
then a fall?

I'd call him every day.
Hola Papa I'd say.
Hola he'd say back,
sure, strong, like
the old days, as if
he weren't dying.

*How goes it
on the western front?*
I'd say, and he'd say—
but now I can't remember.
Was it *okay* or *fine*
or *pretty good, I guess?*

I want to believe
I'll always remember
his voice, even if
the morning comes
when I can't hear him
saying my name.

Caught in the Light

First morning out of bed,
fever finally spent,
I seek sun's warmth,
the sweet smell of new grass.

But days of wild rain
bind this cold slate June.
I move slow, hunched
against the damp,
feet wet in ragged puddles.

Still wings, wide as my hand,
dense with a calligrapher's scrawl,
stop my steps. Near the porch,
in a place I'd seen but never seen,
five dragon flies hide beneath
the sand cherry's purple leaves.

Their long-drawn bodies,
brilliant blue, carry the forgotten sky.
I stand motionless, caught
in the cathedral light
of silent wings.

Just for the Taking

I spend the morning picking beans,
on my knees in a broad farm field.

Incense of warm wet dirt embraces me,
greets me like a prayer. My hands seek,

reach beneath green leaves, remembering
some Braille I didn't know I knew. Inside

the shade sanctuary, purple beans hang
in rows, like sunlight through stained glass.

My mind slows, releases its to-do's, fills
with cricket song, with the steady snap-snap

of beans becoming mine. My silver bucket shines
in the sun, fills with beans, spills over

with beans, just for the taking. One row over,
hundreds of bees waste no time, plunge deep

into white flowers of radish going-to-seed.
A bright yellow grasshopper rides a thin leaf

in the slight wind, his black glassy eye
watches over everything.

My Best Kite Ever

With sticks and strings and careful glue,
I'd made the kite myself. After school,
I took my time, knotted a fine tail, waded

into the wide alfalfa sea behind our house.
Strong west wind caught it, climbed it, circled
it high. String spun out, burned past

my fingers—but I didn't care. String,
two whole balls worth, tied to a stick,
bucked in my hands, nearly got away—

but I held on. Afternoon tipped to evening
but I did not let go. This was my best kite ever.

Then, gone too far, I couldn't pull it back,
tried to wind it on the stick, but it slipped
and slipped. I held on for a long time,

traveled the perfect arc between us, felt it
live through my hand. Far away,
yet near, it rode the dusky night.

I held on as long as I could
and then—I let it go.

Not Gone

My husband stood in the kitchen
and poured the orange juice.

Morning sun pooled around his feet,
bare on the wooden floor.

Your father may be dead,
he said, *but he's not really gone.*

I hadn't thought of that before.

**

For forty years after he died,
Queen Victoria laid out
her husband's clothes. Each night

she soothed the sleeve of his shirt,
buttoned that one button, touched
the scarf that had touched his neck,

tending the ghost
we all must tend.

**

I walk down the hall, hear the scuff
of Father's slippers. He retrieves
the morning paper, first thing—
before coffee, before Grape-Nuts,
before turning on the radio.

I see him at the front door, bent down,
brown corduroy bathrobe, still
in good shape, though mother made it
long ago. I see the backs
of his slippers, the rundown heels.

As If

Three terracotta pots squat on the back steps,
geraniums bloom and bloom as if

it is still summer, as if frost
isn't coming, as if wind

will not rip leaves from all the trees.
White birch flickers under the cobalt sky,

shadows play on the still-green grass.
Peach tree leaves hang

like crescent moons in the October sky.
Old ginger cat basks in the warm sun,

eyes closed, paws at rest, as if
all this—will last forever.

Additional Acknowledgments

Many thanks to Andrea Rexilius, Andrea Hollander, John Brehm and Harrison Candelaria Fletcher for their invaluable advice and inspiration. Thanks also to Elizabeth Robinson and Chris Ransick, my mentors in the Poetry Book Project at the Lighthouse Writer's Workshop, for encouragement and wisdom. Special thanks to Connie Zumpf, Kirsten Morgan, Diane Alters, Lois Levinson, Gail benEzra and Harriet Stratton for support all along the way. Deep gratitude to my family, especially Don and Stephen, for everything.

I am also very indebted the many other mentors, teachers and friends, too numerous to mention, who believed in me, showed me how to take the next step and made this book possible.

Erika D. Walker's writing has been published in *Literary Mama, Pulse: Voices from the Heart of Medicine, Bird's Thumb, The Human Touch: Journal of Poetry, Prose and Visual Art* and *Medical Literary Messenger*. She co-authored *Denver Mountain Parks: 100 Years of the Magnificent Dream* which won a Colorado Book Award. She serves as a judge for the Colorado Book Awards and is a graduate of the Poetry Book Project at the Lighthouse Writer's Workshop in Denver, Colorado.

www.ingramcontent.com/pod-product-compliance
Lightning Source LLC
LaVergne TN
LVHW041511070426
835507LV00012B/1483